THE
SECRET LIFE
OF DOGS

Out of the Wild and Into Our Homes

Jackie Brown

NATIONAL
GEOGRAPHIC

WASHINGTON, D.C.

Dogs such as this golden retriever puppy have learned how to live peacefully with a completely different species—us.

Previous pages: Unlike their wolf relatives, modern dogs are driven to connect with humans.

I CONTENTS

CHAPTER ONE

FROM WOLF TO WOOF 6

Thousands of years ago, as dogs evolved from wolves, their role changed from wild predators into our invaluable helpers and close friends.

CHAPTER TWO

THE HUMAN-DOG BOND 40

As humans fine-tuned their choice of primitive hunting dogs to create highly specialized working breeds, dogs eventually moved indoors, becoming cherished family members.

CHAPTER THREE

INSIDE DOG BEHAVIOR 68

Research into how dogs think and act has led to a greater understanding of this animal species living in a human world.

INTRODUCTION

Loving and learning from our best friends

Even though dogs were the very first animal species humans domesticated, and they have become an integral part of our day-to-day lives, much about the origins of the domestic dog remains a mystery. We know dogs evolved from wolves, but we still don't know exactly where, when, and how dogs changed into the friendly, helpful animal companions we know and love.

Perhaps because dogs are so beloved, scientists are passionate about finding answers regarding their beginnings. New research is continually being published; some studies offer revelations while others contradict previous findings. Every discovery brings us one step closer to finally revealing the origins of humankind's best friend.

Dogs have been living alongside people for thousands of years, learning how to get along with us, a completely separate species that operates by very different rules. Likewise, humans

DID YOU KNOW?

A DOG'S **NOSEPRINT** **IS AS UNIQUE** AS A HUMAN FINGERPRINT.

Playful Marley, a beloved mutt who was rescued from a shelter at eight weeks old, lived to see his 15th birthday.

Dogs remain invaluable helpers to the Nenets people (above), nomadic reindeer hunters who live in the Siberian high Arctic.

are often mystified by dog behavior, making it hard to prevent and correct problems as they arise. Luckily, experts know a lot about dogs' physiology and behavior, which offer glimpses inside their secret lives. Dogs might not speak, but by understanding canine behavior and body language, we can interpret what they are thinking and feeling, and why they act the way they do.

Despite differences between dogs and humans, we have come together in incredible ways. At first, humans valued dogs for their hunting and guarding skills, and dogs appreciated the easy food they received from people. Over time, dogs became equally valued for their companionship, and science seems to show that they love us for more than the simple fact that we feed them. Working dogs still help humans in important ways, but first and foremost our dogs provide undeniable friendship, comfort, cuddles, and love. ◉

CHAPTER ONE

FROM WOLF TO WOOF

THE EVOLUTION AND BIOLOGY OF DOGS

Arctic wolves scavenge
a musk ox carcass on
Ellesmere Island, Canada.
Scientists study modern
and ancient wolves to learn
more about domestic dogs.

DOGS THEN AND NOW

Understanding the past gives clues to our present

Dogs have always been special. They are not only humankind's best friend but also our oldest. The familial relationship we share is even echoed in the domestic dog's scientific name: *Canis lupus familiaris.* Wolves *(Canis lupus),* once predatory threats to humans and competitors for shared food sources, eventually evolved to become partners, protectors, and friends. But when, where, and how did dogs evolve?

The fact is, we don't yet have definitive answers to these questions. Though theories abound, scientists don't agree on who domesticated dogs or where they did it. The exact timing of the appearance of the domestic dog is hotly debated, but based on the latest science, it most likely falls somewhere between 15,000 and 40,000 years ago. A 2022 study that analyzed the DNA of 72 ancient wolves from Europe, Siberia, and North America over a span of 100,000 years suggests that canine domestication occurred on

DID YOU KNOW?

DOGS SLEEP AN AVERAGE OF **12 TO 14 HOURS A DAY.**

Cave paintings, such as this one in Algeria, depict dogs hunting with humans and offer a glimpse of early life with domesticated dogs.

Much about the evolution of the domestic dog remains a mystery, but one thing we know for certain is that dogs came from wolves, changing drastically along the way (opposite).

the earlier side, as far back as 40,000 years ago. The huge study concluded that dogs are most closely related to ancient wolves from eastern Eurasia, but it also found evidence of dual domestication events, possibly in East Asia and the Middle East.

Evidence of Dog Evolution

The one thing everyone agrees on is that dogs evolved from wolves. The appearance of domestic dogs predates written language, so researchers initially relied on archaeological evidence to support theories of dog evolution. Fossil evidence suggested that dogs came from wolves, and the first analysis of dog and wolf DNA, carried out in 1997, confirmed it.

Archaeologists and researchers long believed that dogs descended from the gray wolf specifically, and dogs and gray wolves do share 99.9 percent of their DNA. However, the latest research suggests that dogs may be descended from a different, as yet unknown and now extinct, wolf subspecies. In 2021, a new study pointed to the Japanese wolf as the closest relative to modern dogs. This subspecies of the gray wolf has been extinct since 1905 (researchers were able to extract DNA from museum specimens), and likely migrated from East Asia. For all the genomic progress toward understanding dogs' origins, their originating ancestor remains to be found. ◉

Dogs and wolves are so closely related that they can breed together, resulting in dog-wolf hybrids, such as the one seen in the foreground; these usually retain mostly wolf temperaments and physical traits.

Though wolves and dogs look similar, behaviorally the two species are very different. Here, two Arctic wolves are silhouetted in a Canadian sunset.

DOG'S CLOSEST LIVING RELATIVE

The closest living kin to the dog is *Canis lupus*, the gray wolf, also called the timber wolf (below). Many subspecies of gray wolf are found in North America and Eurasia, and one gray wolf subspecies lives in Africa, the African wolf. Despite the name, these canids also come in brown, red, black, or white hues.

Gray wolves live and hunt in packs, forming strong social bonds and working cooperatively for mutual benefit. One male and one female lead their pack, which consists mostly of their offspring, helping it to run smoothly and peacefully.

Colonial farmers and ranchers of the 1800s, who saw wolves as threats to their domestic livestock, began baiting, trapping, and hunting them in great numbers. By about 1950, almost no wolves remained in the continental United States, and by 1978, nearly all wolf subspecies were listed on the U.S. endangered species list. There has, however, been a

reversal in public sentiment, and a new focus on the preservation of these majestic creatures in the wild. In the mid 1990s, biologists captured gray wolves from Canada and rereleased them in Yellowstone National Park and Idaho as part of a wolf restoration project.

CLUES IN CANINE FOSSILS

Using new technology to help solve an ancient riddle

Evolution of the domestic dog took place over a long period of time, during which wolves and dogs continued to interbreed—this muddies the waters when it comes to analyzing canid fossils and even DNA. In considering canine fossils, researchers examine their morphological features, such as size and arrangement of the teeth, size and length of the snout and mandibles, and skull shape. The researchers then compare them to modern dogs, modern wolves, confirmed early dog fossils, and prehistoric wolf fossils.

Some features of ancient dog fossils include short skulls and snouts, crowded and smaller teeth (due to the shortened snouts), and wide palates and craniums. Additionally, scientists can use an advanced bone-measuring technique called geometric morphometrics to analyze the curves of a skull so individual specimens can be more easily compared to each other.

It's not always easy to determine exactly what these bones are. Some Ice Age wolf-dog fossils are classified as "incipient dogs," meaning they are in the early, transitional stages of development—not quite wolf, not quite domesticated dog, but somewhere in between. These incipient dog fossils are more like wolf-dog hybrids, the earliest ancestors of domestic dogs. The oldest of these on record, a large skull, was unearthed in a cave in Goyet, Belgium, in the 1860s. According to radiocarbon dating, the ancient fossil is nearly 36,000 years old. Belonging to what is considered to be a Paleolithic dog, the Goyet dog skull more closely resembles prehistoric dogs than modern wolves.

Radiocarbon dating and an anatomical analysis of another fossil skull, one discovered in a cave in the Altai Mountains of Siberia in 1975, places it at approximately 33,000 years old.

DID YOU KNOW?

DOGS WERE BURIED WITH DEAD RULERS **TO PROTECT THEM FROM HARM** IN THE AFTERLIFE.

Once swaddled as mummies, the remains of a dog and two bulls are displayed at the Agricultural Museum in Cairo (above).

Radiocarbon dating sets the Goyet dog skull (opposite) at nearly 36,000 years old—the oldest doglike skull ever discovered.

Researchers concluded that this doglike skull found in Siberia came from an incipient dog in the early, transitional stages of development.

Part of the Family

We can learn a lot about the relationship between ancient humans and dogs from analyzing dog fossils. For instance, the oldest confirmed dog fossil, known as the Bonn-Oberkassel dog, is believed to be a little over 14,000 years old. The dog's remains, along with those of a man and a woman, were found in 1914 in an ancient grave in Oberkassel, Germany. The Bonn-Oberkassel dog was, in fact, a puppy, about seven months old.

A recent examination of this fossil concluded that the dog suffered from distemper, and that humans provided care and nursed it through bouts of illness before it died. This fossil is also the oldest confirmed evidence of a domestic dog burial with humans. Whether buried alone, with other dogs, or with humans, dog burials indicate a closeness between

dogs and humans that goes beyond keeping an animal for its functional uses. It signifies a high level of regard and hints at the dog's eventual transition from wild animal to pampered pet.

In the 1970s, the skeletal remains of three domestic dogs were unearthed at an archaeological site called Koster, in the Illinois River Valley near the Illinois–Missouri border. The bones were discovered in shallow pits, suggesting they were buried deliberately. Because no tool marks were found on the bones (which would indicate they were killed by humans), the dogs are believed to have died from natural causes. Subsequent radiocarbon dating revealed the Koster dog bones were 10,000 years old.

Beating these out for the title of oldest domestic dog fossil in North America is a 10,150-year-old bone fragment found

DOGS INSTINCTUALLY SLEEP CURLED UP TO **PROTECT THEIR VITAL ORGANS** AND KEEP THEMSELVES WARM.

in Alaska. Though the bone was initially thought to be from an ancient bear, DNA proved it was from a domestic dog. Further analysis of this fossil revealed it to be closely related to a canine ancestor that lived in Siberia 23,000 years ago. All this suggests that Siberian hunters from the Ice Age may have domesticated dogs, and that humans—and their canine companions—migrated to North America from Siberia some 4,000 years

These 10,000-year-old skeletal remains of a domestic dog were uncovered in the Illinois River Valley.

earlier than previously believed, before the glaciers melted. By tracing how dogs moved, we understand more how humans moved.

Looking even further back, researchers analyzed previously sequenced mitochondrial dog genomes and found that all ancient American dogs may have origins traced back to a common canine ancestor that lived in Siberia about 23,000 years ago. Ancient dogs living in North America all but vanished after a few thousand years; this was likely due to the Europeans arriving to the Americas with their own breeds, which quickly took over.

THE CANINE FAMILY TREE

The taxonomic family Canidae includes 12 genera and 36 living species, including *Canis lupus familiaris*—the domesticated dog. Species in the Canidae family are found on every continent except Antarctica. Dogs' closest relatives are those in the same genus, *Canis,* which includes various species of wolves, coyotes, jackals, and dingoes (*Canis lupus dingo*).

GENUS	SPECIES
Vulpes	True foxes (including red foxes)
Canis	Coyotes, dingoes, dogs, jackals, and wolves
Lycalopex	South American foxes
Urocyon	Gray foxes
Atelocynus	Small-eared zorros
Cerdocyon	Crab-eating foxes
Chrysocyon	Maned wolves
Cuon	Dholes
Lycaon	African hunting dogs (African wild dogs, below)
Nyctereutes	Raccoon dogs
Otocyon	Bat-eared foxes
Speothos	Bush dogs (savannah dogs)

Where Did Dogs Come From?

Various studies have focused on three main geographic regions—Asia, the Middle East, and Europe—as places of origin for domesticated dogs. Some scientists believe dogs may have been domesticated twice, in different geographic locations, while others think domestication was a singular event. Science has not yet conclusively identified exactly where dogs originated, but every new study brings us one step closer to solving the mystery.

Ancient doglike fossils found in Belgium and Siberia, as well the Czech Republic—all estimated between 36,000 and 33,000 years old—could imply more than one instance of attempted domestication of wolves, in multiple geographic locations. A few DNA-based studies have also suggested dual lineage, including a large 2022 study that analyzed ancient wolf DNA and found evidence that two domestication events may have taken place in East Asia and the Middle East.

Other research, including two studies published in 2021, has shown evidence of one place of origin for the domesticated dog, one that traced dog origins back to Siberia 23,000 years ago, and one that identified the extinct Japanese wolf as the subspecies most closely related to domestic dogs, suggesting that the ancestor of domestic dogs may have lived in East Asia.

Digging Into Dog DNA

Though scientists have made great strides investigating the evolution of the domestic dog, much of the research is contradictory. We still don't know exactly when wolves became dogs, nor is there a consensus on where domesticated dogs originated.

Mitochondrial DNA analysis, which uses a highly sensitive technique to look at a specific type of DNA found in ancient fossils, has opened a new world of information for researchers trying to pinpoint a time frame for the origin of the modern dog. Because dogs and gray wolves share 99.9 percent of their DNA, researchers can analyze genetic variations. However, DNA analysis is not always clear-cut, making it hard to reach definitive conclusions. It's also tough to use observable traits (such as body size, hair length and color, head and leg shape) within individuals of a species—characteristics called phenotypes—to compare today's dogs with their ancestors, a still unknown subspecies of the gray wolf.

SEQUENCING THE DOG GENOME

A genome is the complete set of DNA instructions needed to build and grow an organism. The dog genome, which has approximately 2.5 billion DNA base pairs, is similarly sized to the human genome (which has about three billion DNA base pairs).

In 2005, a female boxer named Tasha (right) was the first dog genome sequenced by the Canine Genome Sequencing Project, led by the Broad Institute of MIT and Harvard. The boxer was chosen out of 60 dog breeds as it has the least variation in its genome, so it can be used as a reference for all other dog breeds. Other breed genomes have subsequently been sequenced, including that of the ancient basenji, which was sequenced in 2021.

By comparing Tasha's genome to other breeds as well as other species—including humans—scientists can uncover useful information about how genes influence phenotypes, diseases, and more.

The Dog10K Consortium, an international collaboration among researchers, intends to generate whole genomes from 10,000 canids, including 300 different dog breeds from all over the world, encompassing semi-feral dogs that live in and around human habitations as well as niche populations, ancient breeds, and wild canids, including wolves. The project will culminate with a fine-scale, worldwide genomic map for established dog breeds as well as dogs of mixed lineage.

This painted wooden sarcophagus documents the close ties of the ancient Egyptians to their domesticated dogs.

Though fossil evidence points to dog domestication happening around 14,000 years ago, DNA-based research often puts the split between wolves and dogs much earlier. The 2022 DNA study, which analyzed 72 ancient wolf genomes spanning 100,000 years, concluded that dogs likely appeared as long ago as 40,000 years, which roughly lines up with time frames some earlier studies pinpointed. In 2017, for example, researchers analyzed genomes from three ancient dog fossils from Germany and Ireland. After comparing those ancient genomes with genetic data from more than 5,000 modern dogs and wolves, the team estimated that dogs and wolves parted ways between 37,000 and 41,000 years ago. That study also determined that dogs split into two populations between 17,000 and 24,000 years ago: eastern (the progenitors of East Asian breeds) and western (which would go on to become modern European, South Asian, Central Asian, and African breeds). Based on these time frames, they estimate dog domestication occurring sometime between 20,000 to 40,000 years ago.

Science and technology continue to provide new and improved resources for researchers to employ in their search for answers. The more we investigate, the more we will discover about the origins of the dog. ◉

HOW WERE DOGS DOMESTICATED?

The path to becoming humankind's best friends

There are two generally accepted hypotheses about how the domesticated dog emerged. One theory holds that early humans either captured and tamed wolf puppies, or formed relationships with curious scavenging wolves, eventually training the least timid ones to assist with hunting and guarding. In essence, this theory presents people as taking the lead role in domesticating dogs when humans were primarily hunter-gatherers. Several recent DNA-based studies seem to support this theory, placing domestication as long ago as 40,000 years.

Another theory suggests that the shift to an agrarian society was the driving force in dog domestication, as it created an environment where wolves might scavenge food scraps from human settlements and—through repeated interaction with humans—become tamer. Under this theory, domestication occurred after the advent of agriculture, which became more prevalent about 12,000 years ago. Tied into this second theory is the idea that early dog ancestors became able to digest and thrive on a starchy diet, something that makes modern

The Maremma sheepdog (opposite) was developed in the Abruzzo and Maremma regions of Italy, where it has protected sheep from wolves for centuries.

A NEW WAY OF LIFE

After splitting from wolves thousands of years ago and living with humans, dogs such as this Rottweiler (right) evolved to become scavengers rather than hunters. Their bodies adapted to allow them to survive on the foods that were readily available, which included grains and vegetables in addition to meat.

As dogs became closer to humans, eating meat and other food scraps from human settlements, they still retained their hunting instincts. It's possible that early dogs may have helped humans hunt rabbits and other small prey, or even larger animals. Rock art found in Jordan dating to 14,000 years ago depicts dogs driving gazelles into traps called desert kites.

Over time, people in hunter-gatherer societies trained dogs to assist them in hunting, carrying belongings, and providing transportation (as with sled dogs). Humans in turn fed and cared for the dogs, an arrangement that turned out well for both species.

domesticated dogs very different from wolves, which eat a primarily meat-based diet.

Dogs are classified as members of the family Canidae and the order Carnivora. Domesticated cats, which are also members of the order Carnivora, are obligate carnivores (the majority of their diet must be meat), but dogs are considered omnivores. This means that in addition to eating meat, dogs can consume, digest, and extract nutrients from plant-based foods such as grains, fruits, and vegetables. Grains and vegetables are more digestible for dogs when they are cooked. Wolves, on the other hand, are indeed strictly carnivores.

BOTH DOGS AND WOLVES HAVE A **THIRD EYELID** IN THE CORNER OF EACH EYE.

A 2013 genetic analysis looked at DNA from 12 wolves and 60 dogs representing 14 different breeds. The results of this study supported the theory that dietary adaptations allowed the predecessors of modern domestic dogs to thrive on a starch-rich diet of scraps obtained from humans, and that was directly tied to the early domestication of dogs.

High above the fjords of Tasiilaq, Greenland, are two curious Greenland dogs, an ancient sledding dog that is the country's only surviving native breed.

No matter which theory is correct, it's clear that dogs and humans began forming close attachments long ago, setting the stage for thousands of years of cooperation and companionship.

Welcome to the Table

A 2019 study analyzed the remains of 26 ancient dogs found buried in circular graves with other dogs or close to humans near Barcelona, Spain. It determined that the dogs ranged in age from one month to six years old and lived between 3,600 and 4,200 years ago. The dogs were seemingly part of a ceremonial sacrifice.

To explore the relationship between the dogs and humans who lived together at the site, the researchers performed an isotopic analysis of these dog remains, a process that can reveal what an individual ate while it was still living. The results told the scientists that the dogs from the graves ate a similar diet as the humans they were buried with, one high in vegetables and grains, as well as animal protein. This, and the fact that all the adult dogs were similarly sized (and thus similarly nourished), led the researchers to conclude that the dogs were fed with the same food that the humans were eating themselves. People may have fed their dogs rather than allowing the dogs to hunt for themselves so that the dogs could dedicate their time to tasks that helped the humans, likely herding livestock and guarding the settlement.

Ola Magnell, an osteologist (bone scientist), brushes sand from the skeleton of an 8,400-year-old dog at the Blekinge Museum in Sweden.

SURVIVAL OF THE FRIENDLIEST

Transitioning from wild animal to family pet

Although dogs resemble wolves in many ways, the two behave very differently. Wild animals such as wolves have an innate distrust of humans and prefer to avoid contact altogether. Unlike many other domestic species such as cows and sheep, dogs are more than just tame; they demonstrate sociability toward humans—seeking human interaction and seemingly wanting to communicate with us.

In 2017, researchers working with canine DNA found that certain genetic mutations in a region known as the Williams-Beuren syndrome critical region (WBSCR) were strongly associated with dogs' tendency to seek out physical contact from humans and look to humans for help and information. In people, genetic changes in the WBSCR lead to a condition called Williams-Beuren syndrome, which is associated with unique personality traits, including overfriendliness (also called hypersociability).

Other research into the genetics of tameness has focused on a theory that domesticated animals share certain physical and behavioral characteristics. Charles Darwin first described this, noting how domesticated mammals had hereditary traits that did not appear in their wild counterparts. Botanists in the early 1900s applied the theory to plants and gave it the name "domestication syndrome." In dogs, this translates to certain shared characteristics, including the ability to be tamed, loss of seasonally linked reproduction, and physical changes in the ears, tails, head, and coat color.

DID YOU KNOW?

KUBLAI KHAN, AN ANCIENT CHINESE EMPEROR, HAD 5,000 MASTIFFS.

As an example, research has shown that mild neural crest cell deficits can lead to some of the trademark physical and behavioral characteristics we see in domestic dogs, including white spots or a piebald pattern, floppy ears, lowered aggression, and a friendly, trusting disposition. If tameness and physical characteristics shared by domestic dogs are linked, then early humans may have inadvertently changed the physical look of domestic dogs simply by breeding those that showed the most tame and friendly behavior.

Alisa, a fox specially bred at the Institute of Cytology and Genetics in Novosibirsk, Siberia, lives in a home outside of St. Petersburg. She is friendly with her human companions, as well as the family's yellow Labrador retriever.

Taming the Fox

In 1959, Russian geneticist Dmitri Belyaev initiated what became a long-running experiment to study the process of domestication of silver foxes, with a particular interest in how dogs were domesticated from wolves. At the outset, Belyaev and his team evaluated hundreds of fur-farm foxes, choosing the 10 percent with even a tiny hint of tameness for breeding the next generation. The researchers selected foxes based only on tameness— no other criteria were considered.

Within six years (and six generations of foxes), the foxes began exhibiting amazingly doglike behaviors, such as allowing petting and holding, licking people's hands, and even wagging their tails when humans approached. Within 10 years, physical changes were also seen in the foxes, including floppy ears and curly tails, traits described in domestication syndrome theory for dogs. Further on in the experiment, the foxes also developed mottled patterns in their fur and shortened, rounder snouts.

Today, the program is still run by a group of Russian geneticists led by Lyudmila Trut, whose book, *How to Tame a Fox (and Build a Dog)*, authored with biologist Lee Alan Dugatkin, details the experiment and shares lessons learned regarding the evolution of domesticated animals. In recent years, some researchers have challenged the validity of the fox domestication experiment, claiming that the traits attributed to the behavioral selection for tameness were genetically present in the experiment's original 1959 fox population.

In a long-running experiment at the Institute of Cytology and Genetics in Novosibirsk, Siberia, Lyudmila Trut (center) and her staff breed foxes to be as human-friendly as dogs.

A Peruvian archaeologist holds a canine mummy found in a dog cemetery. Ritual burials signify respect for the animal.

Those foxes came from fur farms in eastern Canada and had been captive and purpose-bred since the late 1800s, making them far from wild.

Yet the initial foxes *were* aggressive. The researchers looked for the tiniest hints of tameness when selecting foxes to breed (perhaps, those that growled and bared teeth but didn't launch an attack or bite). Despite its skeptics, the experiment has brought some compelling insights. In 2021, analysis of the brains of 30 foxes from the current farm program found evolved changes to gray matter in the brains of foxes selected for tameness toward humans.

The Rise of Domesticated Dogs

Over time, dogs began helping different cultures of humans with more than just hunting and were used as guard dogs, watchdogs, and war dogs. In ancient Egypt, dogs were valued as working animals and pets. Domestic dog mummies have been discovered buried in tombs alongside their owners, so they could be together in the afterlife. Dogs and other animals were also sometimes mummified as offerings to the gods, especially to Anubis, the Egyptian god of mummification, depicted as possessing the body of a man and a canine head.

Ancient Greece hosted a powerful and ferocious breed known as the Molossus, which were revered guardians. The Romans inherited these massive working dogs from the Greeks and likely employed them as guard dogs and war dogs for the Roman army. Although the Molossus and similar breeds are now extinct, they are probable ancestors of today's mastiff breeds, including the cane corso, mastiff, Neapolitan mastiff, and dogue de Bordeaux.

In ancient Asia, dogs were held in high regard as pets and as hunting dogs, guard dogs, and watchdogs. In Tibet, small, flat-faced dogs would perch on monastery walls, scanning for intruders and sounding the alarm when someone approached. In China, ancestors of breeds such as the Pekingese, pug, and shih tzu were prized companions of royalty. Rather than being relegated to a place on the floor, these tiny dogs were carried around inside their owners' voluminous sleeves, leading to their nickname "sleeve dogs."

Dog ownership in Great Britain and Europe soared during the Middle Ages and through the Renaissance. The leisured classes kept dogs as pets and used them for specialized hunting, including fox hunting, rabbit hunting, and hawking. These prized dogs often slept by the hearth or in a kennel building. Lower classes kept dogs that "earned their keep," whether hunting for game to feed the family or guarding the home. Dogs are frequently included in portraits from this time, providing a glimpse of what they looked like hundreds of years ago.

Many of the modern breeds we know and love today were created or refined during the Victorian era. Queen Victoria loved dogs and had multiple canine companions throughout her long reign, including spaniels, greyhounds, dachshunds, collies, and pugs. Her many subjects followed suit. ◉

WHAT MAKES A DOG A DOG?

Diverse physical characteristics across many breeds

At first glance many dogs—especially certain breeds such as Siberian huskies, Alaskan malamutes, and even German shepherds—still closely resemble wolves. But dogs evolved to have distinct physical characteristics that set them apart. Although physical features vary greatly among dog breeds, dogs in general have rounder heads, shorter muzzles, smaller jaws, and larger eyes than wolves. Wolves never have floppy ears or curly tails, but many dog breeds do. Dogs also have wider frames, heavier builds, and smaller paws compared to wolves.

Size Matters

Selective breeding for specific characteristics has made the dog one of the most diverse species on the planet. Though wolves do vary in size, with larger wolves found in more northern regions and smaller wolves found in the south, the difference in dogs is much larger. Domestic dogs can weigh just a few pounds (the Chihuahua) or hundreds of pounds (the mastiff), with an example of every other size in between.

Until recently, it was assumed that early in the domestication process, humans chose smaller wolves to keep and breed, and the resulting gene pool

Dogs are one of the world's most genetically diverse species, coming in a wide range of sizes, shapes, colors, and coat types, as evidenced by this Saint Bernard and pug duo.

WOLVES VS. DOGS

Although wolves and dogs share 99.9 percent of their DNA and seem similar at first glance, a closer look reveals differences in their physical bodies and behavior.

WOLF	DOMESTIC DOG
Carnivore	Omnivore
Predator/hunter	Opportunistic scavenger
Wild	Domestic (dependent on humans)
Avoid human contact	Seek out human contact
Yellow or golden eyes (never blue)	Brown or blue eyes
Narrow chest and splayed feet	Broad chest and straight feet
Narrow skull and long muzzle	Broader skull and shorter muzzle
Seasonal estrus (usually in heat once a year, in winter)	Variable estrus (usually in heat twice a year)

A dog walker converses with her pack in Quebec, Canada. Dogs inherit the genes for large and small size from their ancestor, the wolf.

DID YOU KNOW?

DOGS CAN BE **RIGHT-PAWED** OR **LEFT-PAWED.**

led to very tiny breeds such as Yorkshire terriers. However, a study published in 2022 explains that two alleles (alternative forms of a gene that are the result of gene mutation) in a gene called *IGF1-AS,* believed to have a major impact on a dog's size, were present in ancient wolves. A 53,000-year-old Pleistocene Siberian wolf had both variants, but when the scientists looked farther back in history, they could not find evidence of the gene tied to larger sizes in any canid species, including coyotes, jackals, and foxes. This suggests that canids were all small originally, and the second allele evolved to help cold-climate canids like the arctic wolf grow larger so they could survive in a harsh environment.

Today, many physical traits vary widely in dogs. Breeds such as the Scottish deerhound and Great Dane have very long legs, while dwarf breeds, including the basset hound and Cardigan Welsh corgi, have very short legs. Dogs can have rectangular or square body shapes; they can be muscular or lean. Their eyes can be brown or blue, or "odd eyed" (different colors). Dogs come in almost every hue and pattern, from solid to spotted to striped to piebald. Their hair can be short or long, wiry or soft, straight or curly, double coated or single coated. When you look at the variety found in dogs, it truly is incredible that all these traits are possible in just one species. ◉

SUPER SENSES

Specialized traits give dogs a wider world view

Though most dogs no longer live in the wild like their wolf ancestors, domestic dogs retain specialized senses once used to help them survive. Dogs are renowned for their incredible sense of smell, but like people, dogs use all their senses to help them navigate their world. In addition to smell, excellent hearing and eyesight help certain breeds hunt, and their taste and touch allow them to enjoy food—and belly scratches.

Smell

Smell is a dog's most powerful sense. Though humans rely primarily on their eyesight to take in their surroundings, dogs learn more from their noses than from their eyes. To get an idea of how a dog "sees" with its nose, picture a park. A human looking at the park might see some people and dogs, a few leafy trees, and a stretch of grass. A dog can see these things too, but its nose senses much more. Although we might smell strong odors like freshly cut grass, dogs can detect extremely miniscule scents, even those that are very old or have been diluted by rain.

Imagine different-colored scent trails crisscrossing all over the park. One color trail might be from a rabbit that hopped across the grass earlier that morning. The bunny is long gone, but

DID YOU KNOW?

DOGS HAVE 18 MUSCLES CONTROLLING **THEIR EARS.**

its scent is left behind. A double trail of two colors leads down the path where a man and his dog walked last night. Yet another color trail floats through the air, blown by the wind—a cat lounging on the ledge of an open window in a house across the street. Dogs can access a wealth of information via scent that humans cannot.

For this reason, dogs are highly valued for their scenting skills, which enable them to track missing persons, detect the presence of drugs or explosives, and even sniff out diseases like cancer. Dogs can smell things people can't because dogs have many more olfactory receptors in their noses. Humans have about six million olfactory receptors; dogs have more than 300 million. The part of the brain that identifies scents is about 40 times larger in dogs than in humans. Some estimate that dogs' noses are as much as 100,000 times more sensitive than humans' noses.

All dogs have an excellent sense of smell, but dogs with long muzzles have

Dogs' incredible sense of smell—as much as 100,000 times stronger than a human's—allows them to assist conservation efforts, such as this Belgian Malinois searching for grizzly bear scat.

more olfactory receptors than dogs with short muzzles, making breeds such as bloodhounds and German shepherds better smellers than dogs with short snouts (such as boxers and pugs). Some dogs, called scent hounds, have been selectively bred to have better sniffing skills than the average dog. This group includes basset hounds, beagles, bloodhounds, and various coonhounds and foxhounds. Of them all, the bloodhound is considered the supreme sniffer, with specialized body parts to help its nose work even better. When following a trail, the bloodhound's long, droopy ears drag on the ground, stirring up the scent and making it easier to breathe in. In addition, loose skin around its face and neck collects scent, trapping it close to the nose so the dog can smell it better.

Hearing

Hearing is a dog's second most powerful sense. Dogs can hear sounds that humans can't, including high-pitched and faint sounds. Whereas the highest-pitched sound adult humans can hear is about 20,000 hertz (Hz), dogs can hear sounds at 47,000 to 65,000 Hz. Dogs can also detect sounds between -5 and -15 decibels—too quiet for human ears to hear. The ability to hear high pitched as well as soft sounds may date to when dogs hunted for their food, allowing them to hear the squeaking and movements of mice and similar prey.

Sight

Sight is one of a dog's less powerful senses, although they still put their vision to good use. A dog's eyesight is overall poorer than a human's. A person's visual acuity—how clearly and separately we can see objects at a distance—is estimated to be three times greater than that of a dog's. So, something that a human can see clearly at 90 feet away would need to be 30 feet away for a dog to see it as clearly.

Dogs, however, have a wider field of vision than humans because a dog's eyes are more toward the sides of their heads. Some breeds, called sight hounds, have an even greater field of vision than other dogs, including superior panoramic and peripheral vision.

Bloodhounds (opposite) help police by tracking human quarry. The breed's distinctive, loose skin helps the dog follow the trail by capturing scent and keeping it close to the nose.

GET TO KNOW A DOG'S NOSE

Every dog has a unique nose print. Much like human fingerprints, no two dogs' nose prints are the same. A 2021 study found that by the time a beagle puppy is two months old, its nose print is fully formed and will not change over time.

Like humans, dogs have two nostrils but with slits along the sides. Air goes in the round section and out through the slits. This way, the exhaled air doesn't get in the way of incoming smells. And, unlike humans, dogs can use each nostril on its own, each independently of the other. This means a dog can smell one scent with the right nostril and another scent with the left nostril, all at the same time. Research has shown that dogs actually prefer using different nostrils for different scents; unfamiliar scents are explored with the right nostril, and familiar scents with the left.

Though nose color doesn't affect smelling ability, dog noses do come in many different shades, including black (as seen in this Doberman, right), gray (usually referred to as blue), pink, red, and brown (usually called liver)—and even spotted.

Today, dogs still do one of their original jobs—help people hunt. This Labrador retriever waits for a command while a shooter and loader hunt grouse on a Scottish estate.

Physical touch, including cuddling and petting, is one way dogs bond with their humans.

Not surprisingly, sight hounds have been bred to hunt using their extraordinary sight and speed. Examples of this group include the Afghan hound, borzoi, greyhound, Irish wolfhound, pharaoh hound, and Saluki.

Dogs also process visual information 25 percent faster than people do. This explains why dogs are so great at catching balls and Frisbees—compared to what humans see, dogs experience movement in slow motion, giving them plenty of time to get right into position.

Despite popular belief, dogs can see color, although the range of colors dogs perceive is much smaller than what humans see. It's thought that dogs can most easily see blues and yellows, and some studies suggest that dogs view colors similarly to a human who has red-green color blindness.

Taste

Likewise, taste is less refined in dogs than in humans, mainly because dogs have far fewer taste buds than we do (humans have about 9,000 taste buds; dogs have some 1,700). Like humans, dogs can distinguish between sweet, sour, salty, and bitter tastes, and dogs even have specialized taste buds for tasting water—something we do not have—which likely evolved to ensure they remained hydrated. These special water taste buds also become activated at specific times, including after the dog eats a meal. Dogs also have specialized taste receptors for meats and fats. Though dogs can taste salt, they can't detect it as well as other tastes.

Touch

Touch is important for dogs in terms of social interaction and bonding, both with other dogs and with humans. Dogs vary in how much human touch they enjoy or tolerate. Some dogs love being stroked and rubbed, while others prefer only the occasional pat. This may be in part due to individual preference but can also be related to the

Dogs easily pluck fast-moving tennis balls from the air because their rapid visual processing allows them to see movement in what humans would regard as slow motion. Cesar Millan watches the play.

amount of socialization a dog received as a puppy.

Dogs also feel things via their paw pads, which are made of thick, tough skin. A dog's paw pads can be softer or tougher depending on how much time they spend outdoors navigating rough terrain. Though a dog's paw pads essentially act like shoes, allowing them to walk over hard surfaces, they are not invincible—the pads can become cut by rocks, burned by hot ground temperatures, and even frostbitten in freezing conditions. Dogs that go outdoors on hot asphalt or in snow should wear dog booties to protect their feet. ◉

CHAPTER TWO

THE HUMAN-DOG BOND

LIFE AND LOVE WITH OUR CANINE COMPANIONS

In remote places, canines such as this sled dog not only provide transportation but also promote mental health by offering love and companionship.

BRED ON PURPOSE

Breeding with an emphasis on a dog's specialized skills

Starting around the Middle Ages, humans began breeding highly specialized working dogs in earnest. As it turned out, predatory behavior in dogs could be modified so that dogs retained their drive to stalk, chase, and catch and carry prey—but not kill it, tear it apart, or eat it. Breeding for specialized skills allowed specific types of dogs to evolve, including hunting hounds, herding dogs, and bird dogs.

Stalking behavior transformed into pointing at birds. Chase and carry behaviors led to retrievers with "soft mouths" that don't crush birds fetched for a human hunter. Herding dogs both stalk and chase but do not attack or kill. Some dogs, including terriers, were bred to retain the "kill" part of the predatory sequence, becoming ratters to do away with vermin plaguing humans.

Companion dogs also emerged, cherished primarily for their sweet temperaments and cuddly tendencies. Written documentation traced as far

back as the Tang dynasty in China (A.D. 618 to 907) is evidence that lapdogs were gifted to Chinese royalty and kept strictly for companionship. Prior to about the 18th century, companion dogs were generally kept by nobility and royalty, but by the Victorian era, lapdogs became popular among all classes, mostly kept as pets by women and children.

Modern Working Dogs

Although many pet dogs today no longer perform the jobs for which they were originally developed, some breeds continue to do specialized jobs. These dogs are as likely to be found working as hanging out inside the house.

In Chile, dogs help workers as they take sheep into a shearing shed. Shepherds may use up to a dozen dogs trained to respond to whistles, gestures, and shouts.

After being wounded in battle, Layka, a Belgian Malinois deployed to Afghanistan as a trained military dog, was adopted by Staff Sergeant Julian McDonald, a member of Layka's team (opposite).

DID YOU KNOW?

IN THE UNITED STATES, **69 MILLION HOUSEHOLDS** OWN AT LEAST ONE DOG.

High-energy, intense herding breeds such as Australian cattle dogs, Australian kelpies, Belgian Malinois, and border collies continue to be employed to herd sheep, cattle, goats, and other livestock on ranches and farms. Large breeds known for their watchfulness and protective tendencies, such as Anatolian shepherds, Great Pyrenees, komondor, and kuvasz, are also commonly used on farms and ranches to guard livestock, protecting them from predators and thieves.

Many different breeds still hunt with humans, including various pointers, retrievers, spaniels, setters, hounds, and terriers. Several breeds are commonly trained for police and military work, chosen for their agility, stamina, and ease in training. These breeds include bloodhounds, Dutch shepherds, German shepherds, and Labrador retrievers.

In the northern climes of Alaska and Canada, Alaskan malamutes, Chinooks, Samoyeds, and Siberian huskies—which evolved over thousands of years and were used to aid in communication and transportation—are commonly found competing in dogsled racing events, also called mushing. Such breeds are known as spitz breeds or northern breeds. Most have heavy double coats to protect them from the cold. ◉

Rangers use highly trained dogs to track down wildlife poachers at Manyara Ranch, a conservancy north of Tanzania's Tarangire National Park.

Salukis, sight hounds known as some of the fastest dogs in the world, are able to sprint more than 40 miles an hour.

THE OLDEST DOG BREEDS

Some breeds were created relatively recently, in the last two hundred years or so, but others have roots that go much further back. No one knows for sure exactly which breed is the oldest, but a few are in the running, including the following:

Basenji: Known as the "African barkless dog," the basenji lived in Africa for thousands of years. Prehistoric cave paintings found in Libya and dated between 6000 B.C. and A.D. 100 depict hunting scenes with dogs that look similar to basenjis. Though they do not bark like other dogs, basenjis are vocal, their repertoire including an unusual *baroo* sound often described as a yodel.

Dingo: The dingo, Australia's wild dog, is thought to have been brought to that country from Asia thousands of years ago. Radiocarbon dating of the oldest dingo bones yet found, discovered in Australia in 1969, are between 3,348 and 3,081 years old.

New Guinea singing dog: Genetically similar to the dingo, this rare dog (right) may still be found in the wild on the island of New Guinea, north of Australia. Named for its unique vocalizations—described as a cross between a wolf's howl and a whale song—the New Guinea singing dog was thought to have arrived on the island about 3,500 years ago.

Saluki: This breed originated in the Middle East where ancient images of dogs resembling the Saluki, including in tomb paintings, date back at least 5,000 years. This swift sight hound was sacred to the ancient Egyptians who used them to hunt gazelles.

SHOW-OFFS

Bragging rights for enthusiasts of all dog breeds

Over time, breeds were developed or evolved naturally in various geographical regions, with many later becoming extinct or enveloped into other types of dogs. By the 1800s, a huge number of new dog breeds had been developed or refined, many of which are still around today. Breeding the very best working dogs took a lot of effort, and owners would boast about their dogs' prowess as a matter of standing and prestige. Landowners and the very wealthy kept immense kennels to house their packs of hounds and other hunting dogs, maintaining written breeding records.

As a natural evolution, organized dog shows came on the scene. At these shows, breeders—mostly men—would come together to present their animals for judging, winning prizes and bragging rights. They also earned money from the sale of dogs and through stud fees for their prized males.

In Britain, where livestock shows were already commonplace, the first-ever dog show took place in Newcastle as a side event to a popular poultry show in 1859. The Sporting Dog Show was open only to setters and pointers. Sixty exhibitors competed for a pair of double-barreled shotguns donated by a local gunsmith.

Later that year, a dog show that included non-sporting breeds was held in Birmingham, England. It met with such success that when the newly formed Birmingham Dog Show Society held the first National Dog Show the following year, there were 267 entries from 30 breeds. Breeds were loosely grouped by type and skill set (for example, pointers, setters, spaniels, hounds, herding

DID YOU KNOW?

DOGS **SWEAT ONLY FROM THEIR PAWS,** AND HAVE TO COOL DOWN BY PANTING.

This miniature poodle's hairdo is a nod to the breed's hunting heritage—clipped short on the body to make swimming easier but left longer on the chest, hips, and joints to keep vital body parts warm.

Show dogs and their handlers (opposite) become closely connected while training and competing.

dogs, mastiffs, and toy dogs). By the end of the 1860s, the National Dog Show had more than 700 dogs participating—and an excess of 20,000 visitors.

As dog shows proved immensely popular, more began to pop up, both in England and in the United States. The Grand National Exhibition of Sporting and Other Dogs, held in Chelsea, England, in 1863, had more than 1,200 entries. The Kennel Club was founded in England in 1873, and in 1891, the group organized the first Crufts Dog Show in London, which is still held today.

In the United States, the Westminster Kennel Club was established in 1877 and hosted the New York Bench Show of Dogs in New York City that same year. Now called the Westminster Kennel Club Dog Show, the annual occurrence is the country's second longest continuously running sporting event (the Kentucky Derby is the longest running).

Modern Breeding

Breeding and dog shows are still serious business. Today, some 1,500 American Kennel Club (AKC) dog shows take place annually in the United States alone. Tens of thousands of dogs participate, often at high cost to their owners, who pay for training, grooming, handling, travel, and entrance fees (in 2021, this combined total was estimated at $250,000 for attending the Westminster Kennel Club Dog Show).

In addition to bragging rights, stud fees for the winner can bring some income, but this rarely offsets the costs breeders put into their program. The main reason people participate in the "dog fancy," as the hobby is called, is for love of their breed. Dog breeds that have been around for hundreds of years

THE BELOVED MUTT

Though much attention is given to purebreds and designer dogs, more than half of all dogs living in the United States are mixed breeds—the all-American mutt (below). No two are alike, making for uniquely personable companions. In addition to being lovable, mutts—especially those with many different breeds in their background—are usually healthier than purebreds thanks to diversity in their genes that leads to less risk for inherited diseases.

Mixed-breed puppies come largely from unneutered dogs mating, and many end up needing new homes. Of the nearly 3.3 million dogs that enter U.S. animal shelters every year, many are mutts. You can find all sorts of puppies and adult dogs available for adoption through animal shelters and rescue groups. Adoption not only helps save lives but also is less costly than buying a purebred puppy or designer breed.

or longer are still here, due to hobby breeders who participate in dogs shows and make breeding choices that aim to preserve breeds for future generations.

Some breeds look quite different from how they did in the Victorian era, and others have been changed slightly or refined in some ways. But when compared to paintings and illustrations from hundreds of years ago, most breeds are immediately recognizable. Modern dog lovers have been able to preserve these lineages due to breed standards, which are the written description of the ideal breed specimen.

Breed standards are like blueprints, detailing a breed's physical characteristics such as height, weight, body shape, ear type, muzzle length, and coat texture and color, as well as temperament traits and even gait (the way the dog moves). Attention to the breed standard is the reason a golden retriever continues to look like a golden retriever and

a cocker spaniel like a cocker spaniel. Without breed standards, personal preferences and indiscriminate breeding would change a breed over time.

At dog shows, dogs are judged not against each other, but against their own breed standards. The dog that best meets the description of the ideal of that breed is declared the winner. Professional breeders keep careful records and pedigrees (a dog's family tree), mating together only those who both meet the breed standard and complement each other.

Purebred Problems

Purebred dog breeding is not without its controversies. Some believe that certain breeds have been bred to unhealthy extremes, including brachycephalic (flat-faced) breeds, such as the bulldog and pug, and dwarf breeds including

HAIR OF THE DOG

Hundreds of genes interact to produce a physical trait in humans and most mammals. For dog traits, the magic number is usually three or fewer. In the following diagram, the type of coat a dog has depends on the three genes shown below.

Mutations in these genes create a coat that's long, curly, wiry, or a combination. If none of the three genes are mutated, the dog will have the short, smooth coat of breeds like beagles and basset hounds—and the dog's ancestor, the gray wolf.

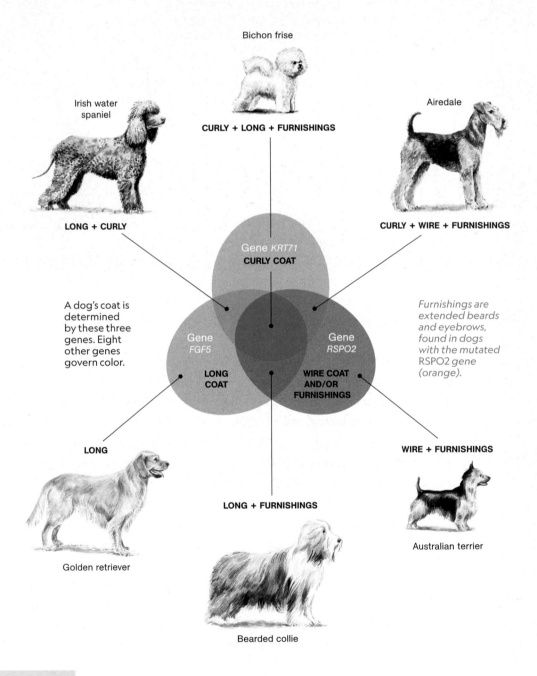

Bichon frise

CURLY + LONG + FURNISHINGS

Irish water spaniel

LONG + CURLY

Airedale

CURLY + WIRE + FURNISHINGS

Gene *KRT71*
CURLY COAT

A dog's coat is determined by these three genes. Eight other genes govern color.

Gene *FGF5*

LONG COAT

Gene *RSPO2*

WIRE COAT AND/OR FURNISHINGS

Furnishings are extended beards and eyebrows, found in dogs with the mutated RSPO2 gene (orange).

LONG

LONG + FURNISHINGS

WIRE + FURNISHINGS

Australian terrier

Golden retriever

Bearded collie

JOHN TOMANIO, NGM STAFF. DOG ILLUSTRATIONS: DAN WILLIAMS
SOURCE: ADAM BOYKO, CORNELL UNIVERSITY

Dogs such as the poodle and Bichon frise (above), with coats that continually grow, need regular haircuts, either from a professional groomer or at home.

the basset hound and dachshund. In 2022, Norway banned the breeding of bulldogs and cavalier King Charles spaniels, citing their inherent health problems, among them breathing issues for the former and heart issues for the latter.

Most purebred dogs have one or more inherited health issues known in the breed. Responsible breeders work hard to breed out genetically linked health problems such as hip and elbow dysplasia, eye issues, heart defects, and other diseases so future generations are healthier. Many genetic tests and health screenings are available to check for these difficulties; reputable breeders test their adult dogs for known genetic issues before breeding

DID YOU KNOW?

IN 2014, THE WESTMINSTER DOG SHOW **ALLOWED MUTTS TO COMPETE FOR THE FIRST TIME—** IN THE AGILITY COMPETITION.

them, avoiding those carrying genes for certain problems.

Although these diagnostic tools have helped improve the overall health of many purebred dogs, some people feel the standards and conformity that breeders and breed clubs promote need to be reevaluated to further prioritize dogs' health. ◉

AKC GROUPS

The American Kennel Club (AKC), which was founded in 1884, maintains a registry of purebred dogs in the United States and offers competition events, including conformation dog shows and performance sports like agility, obedience, field trials, and scent work. The AKC classifies dog breeds by original purpose into seven groups:

Sporting: Dogs in this group are mostly used to hunt birds by pointing, flushing, and retrieving. Examples include retrievers such as the golden retriever, Labrador retriever, flat-coated retriever, and the Nova Scotia duck tolling retriever, which acts as a decoy for duck hunters, frolicking on shore to lure curious ducks in for a closer look.

This group also encompasses spaniels (cocker spaniel, English springer spaniel, Brittany), pointers (English pointer, vizsla, Weimaraner), and setters (English setter, Irish setter, Gordon setter). A different sort of hunter, the curly-coated Italian lagotto Romagnolo, sniffs out truffles, the expensive fungi used in high-end cuisine.

Hound: Dogs in this group hunt via their incredible sense of smell (scent hounds) or sight and speed (sight hounds). Some of the former group include the basset hound, beagle, bloodhound, and dachshund. In the latter category are the long-legged Afghan hound, borzoi, greyhound, and Irish wolfhound.

Working: This group contains dogs bred to guard livestock, pull carts or sleds, and protect property and people. Among these are the imposing boxer, Doberman pinscher, mastiff, Siberian husky, and the Greater Swiss mountain dog which, in addition to other farm duties, once pulled heavy carts loaded with milk and meat to sell at markets. Another popular breed in this group, the massive Newfoundland, originally helped fishermen pull in nets, haul fish to the market, and rescue struggling swimmers.

Herding: Variously called sheepdogs, shepherds, and collies, these high-energy breeds excel at herding livestock. The herding group includes the Australian shepherd, Belgian Malinois, border collie, Cardigan Welsh corgi, and the rough collie, famous for starring as the main character in the book *Lassie Come Home,* which became a popular television series and movie.

Terrier: Dogs in this group are known for their tenacity and ratting skills, such as the cairn terrier, Russell terrier, and Scottish terrier. The Bedlington terrier looks like a sweet little lamb, but is ferocious when in pursuit of its prey. The breed was first used to hunt rats in coal mines in England in the 1800s. Though most terriers originated in Great Britain, the Terrier Group includes a German breed—the miniature schnauzer.

Toy: Dogs in the toy group have one job—that of loving companions. Examples include the Chihuahua (among the category's smallest), Maltese, shih tzu, Yorkshire terrier, and pug (among the group's largest). One of the most unique-looking toy breeds might be the Chinese crested, which is hairless other than poofs on the head, paws, and tail. Many people think the miniature pinscher, affectionately known as the min pin, is a bred-down version of the Doberman pinscher, but the min pin is a much older breed. Both breeds may share a common ancestor (an older breed known as the German pinscher).

Non-Sporting: The Non-Sporting Group is a kind of catchall group for breeds that don't naturally fall into any of the other six AKC groups. Many in this group were bred for very specialized purposes, such as the Dalmatian. This distinctive spotted breed was used as a "coach dog," trotting alongside horse-drawn carriages and wagons—including fire wagons—and protecting them and the horses from thieves. Among other examples are the small and agile Norwegian lundehund, which hunted puffins in Norway by climbing up rocky cliffs, and the long-haired Lhasa apso, which acted as a watchdog in monasteries. Some other breeds in this group include the bulldog, chow chow, keeshond, and schipperke, or "little captain," a small Belgian dog used as a ratter on barges.

CHIHUAHUA

RHODESIAN RIDGEBACK   YORKSHIRE TERRIER

DOBERMAN PINSCHER   STANDARD POODLE

CHESAPEAKE BAY RETRIEVER   DOGUE DE BORDEAUX

54

AFGHAN HOUND   BORDER COLLIE

BRUSSELS GRIFFON   PULI

CHINESE CRESTED

55

DESIGNER DOGS

The rise of doodles and other planned-for mixes

Purebred dogs have been treasured for hundreds of years, with people fiercely devoted to their favorite breeds. But the 1990s saw a new fad—so-called designer dogs.

It all began when Australian breeder Wally Conron was asked to supply a guide dog for a blind woman living in Hawaii. The woman's husband was allergic to dogs. At the time, Conron worked for the Royal Guide Dogs Association of Australia (today called Guide Dogs Victoria). After several failed attempts at training standard poodles as guide dogs, Conron decided to cross a standard poodle with a Labrador retriever.

Three pups in the litter ended up being good candidates for guide dogs, but the husband with allergies could only tolerate one. That dog, named Sultan, was trained and sent off to Hawaii. But the organization had trouble pairing the other two dogs with blind handlers; people wanted purebred Labrador retrievers, not mixed breeds.

Conron asked the group's public relations department to notify the media and share that they had created a brand-new, "nonallergenic" guide dog called the Labradoodle. The gimmick worked and suddenly people were clamoring for this new guide dog breed. When the general public heard of the Labradoodle, people wanted them as

SOME DOG BREEDS **HAVE WEBBED FEET** TO HELP THEM SWIM

pets. Other breeders began crossbreeding Labs and poodles, golden retrievers and poodles, and as the years went on, many other breeds with poodles, making up cutesy names and fueling the "doodle" craze.

Oodles of Doodles

Today, the poodle has been crossed with nearly every breed imaginable, though the Labradoodle and goldendoodle are the most popular. Other designer breeds—such as the puggle (a pug crossed with a beagle) and goldador (a golden retriever crossed with a Labrador retriever)—leave out the poodle and instead combine other breeds.

Along with the beloved mutt, designer dog breeds are not recognized by most breed registries in North America such as the American Kennel Club, Canadian Kennel Club, or United Kennel Club. Unlike purebred dogs, designer dogs do not have officially recognized breed standards. Personal preferences among breeders means the dogs have no standardized look.

The appearance of designer dogs, such as this Labradoodle, are not standardized the way purebred dogs are: size, color, shape, coat, and even temperament can vary wildly.

Poodles are a low-shedding breed, which means fewer allergens such as dander are released into the air.

POODLES WERE BRED TO **RETRIEVE BIRDS FROM LAKES AND PONDS** FOR THEIR HUNTER-OWNERS.

Though many people believe doodles do not trigger dog allergies and don't shed, this is often not the case, especially when the parents of a litter are a poodle and a purebred of another breed. Doodles that are 75 percent poodle and 25 percent another breed are more likely to have the poodle's hypoallergenic coat, though it's not guaranteed. The term "hypoallergenic" means less allergenic, or less likely to cause allergies. No dog—whether purebred, designer, or mixed breed—is guaranteed to not trigger a person with allergies, though some people suffering from allergies to dogs find they can successfully live with certain breeds that are truly hypoallergenic, such as poodles, bichons frises, and Portuguese water dogs.

Today, guide dog programs more commonly use such dogs as Labs, golden retrievers, and German shepherds rather than doodles. Conron has publicly stated that he regrets creating the Labradoodle and laments the health issues seen in dogs indiscriminately bred by those wanting to capitalize on the doodle trend. However, people who love the Labradoodle and other designer breeds see it differently. For better or worse, these designer mixes are probably here to stay. ◉

GROWING CLOSER

Making the move indoors and into our hearts

After spending thousands of years as working animals living outside, dogs eventually made their way into our homes and even our beds. Today, there are an estimated 471 million pet dogs worldwide, with some 68 percent of households in the United States including a dog. Although most dogs in the U.S. spend at least some time indoors, there has been a gradual shift over the last 50 years or so from relegating the family dog to the backyard doghouse to bringing them indoors to live full time with their humans. Many dogs live entirely inside the house.

Pampered and Protected

The move indoors seems to have strengthened the human-canine bond and has made people more aware of and more concerned about their pets' welfare. According to the American Veterinary Medical Association, 85 percent of dog owners think of their pets as family members. As people begin to treat dogs more like children or grandchildren, spending on pet supplies and services has skyrocketed: In 2021, U.S. owners spent $123.6 billion on their pets.

Today's dog owners are also more discerning when it comes to dog food.

CAN'T KEEP MY EYES OFF YOU

There's a biological reason your dog feels like family. Dogs such as this English springer spaniel puppy (below) have evolved to commandeer the human brain's bonding system, something theorized as intended to create strong social connections between adults and children under their care. When looking into each other's eyes, for example, the brains of mothers and babies release a feel-good hormone called oxytocin. Sometimes called the "love" hormone, oxytocin helps create strong feelings of bonding and attachment.

Studies have shown that dogs elicit the same release of oxytocin in their owners' brains, an effect seen most strongly when dog and human gaze deeply into each other's eyes. Dogs also release oxytocin into their own systems when they participate in mutual gazing. Research has found that wolves, even those raised by humans, do not participate in eye gazing and do not cause the same increases in oxytocin when interacting with humans.

It's become standard for people to have their dogs join them on adventures anywhere dogs are allowed.

Gone are the days of kibble from the grocery store's food aisle being their only option. People seek organic or natural ingredients, paying more for premium dog food, or even cooking their own dog food at home. Dogs wear shirts or dresses and fancy collars, and even get "pawdicures" and blueberry facials at the groomer. Instead of being left home alone all day while their owners go elsewhere for work, many dogs head to doggie day care or get a visit by a dog walker for some midday exercise. Nearly half of all dog owners use an electronic tracking device to keep tabs on their pets.

Dogs are such a huge part of our lives that it's not surprising they have become ubiquitous in popular culture. Everyone has their favorite fictional pooch. Whether Lassie, Snoopy, Toto, Old Yeller, or Marley, dogs from books, comics, and movies inspire us, and make us laugh or cry—or sometimes both. ◉

Today, many dogs are valued more for their companionship than for their working skills, but as with people, personality traits vary. Chow chows such as these, for example, usually welcome cuddles only from their human families.

HELPER DOGS

Dogs can benefit our well-being in myriad ways

Dogs give us more than simple love and companionship; they're also good for us. The simple act of living with a dog provides countless physical and emotional health benefits that go beyond the companionship that dogs provide.

Scientific studies have shown that owning a dog lowers blood pressure and lowers the risk of developing cardiovascular disease. Just the common act of petting a dog can lower the body's production of the hormone cortisol, leading to less stress. It makes you more relaxed and can even boost your thinking skills.

The benefits of dog ownership are especially significant for people living alone who have survived heart attacks and strokes—these owners have been found to have a reduced risk of death by repeat episodes compared to people without dogs. Dog owners are also more likely to be active, walking and taking more steps than people without dogs.

Growing up with dogs provides kids with more than the benefits of the human-animal bond. Children exposed to dogs or farm animals early in life have a reduced asthma risk compared with kids who did not live with animals. Another study found that young children who grow up with a dog are less likely to develop Crohn's disease, a common inflammatory bowel disease, possibly because dogs draw their human family members outdoors, which has a correlation to better gut health. As with adults, children who live with dogs also engage in more physical activity and get less screen

FIGHTING CANCER

Genetically, dogs and humans are 95 percent identical, and we are affected by many of the same illnesses, including various types of cancer. A new field called comparative oncology looks at the way cancers affect dogs and humans, and explores different cancer treatments for both species. Researchers seeking better treatments and ultimately cures for common cancers often study dogs, which benefits both dogs and humans.

Scientists might test new cancer drugs in dogs first; if shown to be safe and effective, they move on to human trials, making it a win-win for everyone. As an example, the Morris Animal Foundation is currently funding the Golden Retriever Lifetime Study, one of the largest of its kind in the U.S., with 3,000 golden retrievers enrolled. Its aim is to identify risk factors for cancer and other diseases in dogs. Among all purebred dogs, golden retrievers (right) have the highest incidence of cancer, with 60 percent of all goldens impacted by cancer during their lifetimes. The study's findings may be applied to humans, as well.

Service dogs are permitted by law to accompany their handlers anywhere, even in places not generally considered pet friendly, such as correctional facilities (above).

time than those in households without dogs. Studies have also shown that dog ownership reduces social isolation and loneliness, especially for seniors. People with dogs are more likely to connect socially with others, as well as provide and receive social support.

Most people are familiar with sniffer dogs identifying dangers like explosives and drugs, but dogs can also be trained to alert to almost anything, including cancer and other diseases. In homes, dogs can quickly sniff out harmful termites and bedbugs so they can be promptly exterminated. They can also detect toxic mold hiding inside walls. Dogs are used on farms to note invasive species of agricultural pests and fungal diseases that destroy crops. They can

find invasive fish, reptiles, mammals, and even snails.

Service Dogs

Although most dogs are beloved pets, many are trained to help humans in specific ways—as service dogs, therapy dogs, and emotional support dogs, to name a few. All three are slightly different and afforded varied privileges under the law.

Service dogs are trained to do specific tasks for a person with a disability. Examples include guiding someone who is visually impaired, assisting with balance while walking, retrieving fallen items from the floor, and alerting a person with hearing impairment to a knock at the door. Service dogs attuned

to certain health issues will notify their handler or another person to problems such as an impending seizure, diabetic hypoglycemia, or even an imminent panic attack. Still others are valued for their roles as autism service dogs, psychiatric service dogs, and allergy-detection dogs, which are trained to sniff out ingredients like peanuts or eggs for kids with severe food allergies.

Many service dogs are bred, raised, and trained by specific organizations, whether nonprofit or for-profit. When they are ready, the dogs are paired with a handler in need, and the group provides further training to the dog-handler team. Pet dogs may be trained as service dogs too, especially as medical alert dogs. All service dogs are considered working dogs, and many wear labeled harnesses or vests while out in public to remind people not to pet them as this might distract the dog from their assigned job.

Therapy Dogs

Therapy dogs differ from service dogs as they are not working dogs but are pets that are trained to volunteer to help those in need. Therapy dogs and their handlers visit people in hospitals, nursing homes, airports, disaster sites, and other facilities, bringing comfort and lifting spirits. Large dogs may sit beside

a patient's wheelchair or bed, at a height handy for petting; smaller dogs might be placed on a patient's bed. Some therapy dogs are trained to sit quietly while children read to them, a situation found to be less intimidating than reading aloud to other kids or adults.

Any dog can become a therapy dog. To be trained for therapy work, however, dogs must have the right temperament. Dogs that are calm, gentle, friendly, and confident generally do best. Training includes obedience skills, as well as ensuring the dog is comfortable with medical equipment such as wheelchairs, and unexpected sounds and movements.

Several different national and local organizations offer training and certification for therapy dogs. Most groups require that dogs are at least one year old before becoming certified. After certification, the dog and handler team then volunteer in scheduled shifts at the type of facility they wish to visit.

Guide dogs make it easier and safer for people with visual impairments to navigate around obstacles. The dogs are meticulously trained starting in puppyhood before being matched.

Therapy dogs are not afforded the same access to public spaces as service dogs. Although allowed inside hospitals, nursing homes, and libraries during scheduled volunteer time, they are not guaranteed access to restaurants, stores, planes, or public transportation.

Emotional Support Dogs

Some pets, dubbed emotional support dogs, help people with anxiety, depression, phobias, and other emotional health issues simply with their comforting presence. As with therapy dogs, emotional support dogs do not have the same rights as service dogs to be allowed in public places or to ride in the cabin of airplanes or other public transportation. However, the 1968 Fair Housing Act mandates "reasonable accommodations" for emotional support animals. This includes waiving pet deposits or other fees and allowing emotional support dogs to live in housing that has a no-pets policy. ⦿

SERVICE DOGS AND THE LAW

The Americans with Disabilities Act (ADA), a civil rights law prohibiting discrimination against people with disabilities, outlines specific provisions pertaining to service animals. It defines a service animal as "a dog that is individually trained to do work or perform tasks for a person with a disability."

Under the ADA, state and local governments, businesses, restaurants, and public nonprofit organizations must allow service animals to accompany their handlers. Service dogs are also allowed to fly in the cabin of airplanes and to ride on public transportation such as buses and trains. Service animals are not required to be certified or registered with any organization, and staff may only make limited inquiries when trying to ascertain if a dog is a service animal, including asking what tasks or work the dog has been trained to perform. They cannot ask for any documentation or request that the dog demonstrate the task.

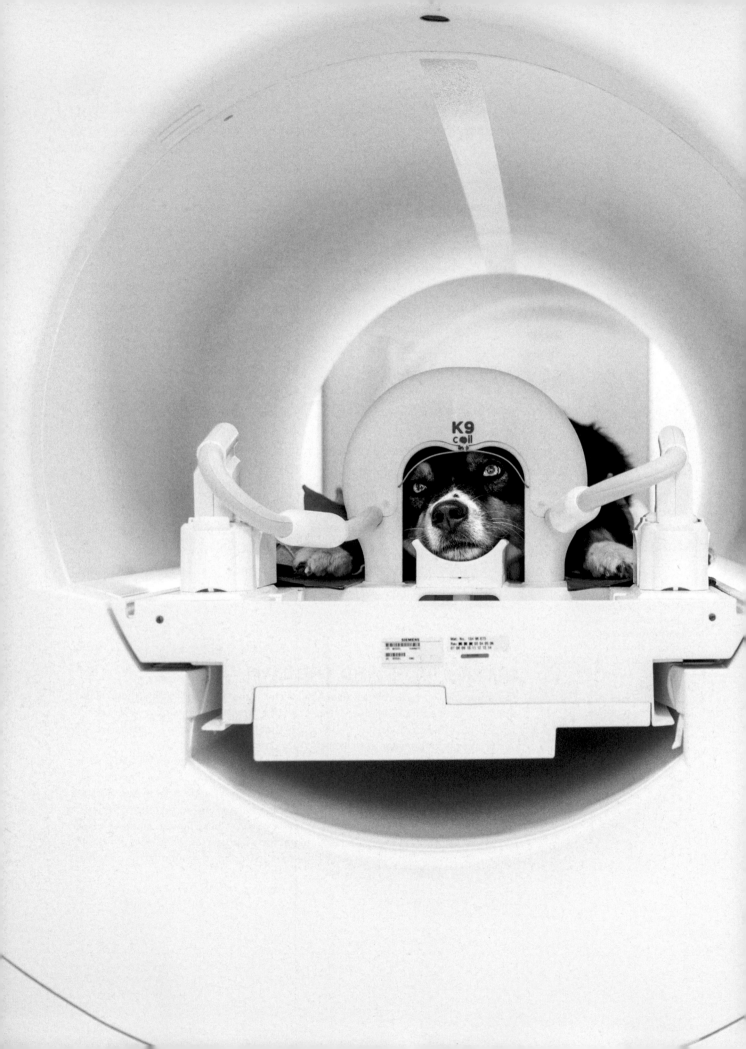

INSIDE DOG BEHAVIOR

WHY THEY ACT THE WAY THEY DO

Dogs such as this Australian shepherd are trained to lie motionless while inside an MRI machine, allowing researchers to study their brains.

DOG SMARTS

Our canine companions can understand more than we may think

Based on our interactions with dogs, it is easy to see that they are an intelligent species—but just how sharp is the average dog? It turns out that dogs can learn words, read human body language, solve problems, discern between thousands of different smells, and comprehend and execute complicated skill sets. The intelligence of an average dog is roughly comparable to that of a two-year-old human child. Some breeds and individual dogs are even smarter, on par with a two-and-a-half- to three-year-old child.

DOGS ARE CAPABLE OF **LEARNING HOUSE-HOLD TASKS,** SUCH AS LOADING A WASHING MACHINE OR RETRIEVING ITEMS BY NAME.

The comparison of dog intelligence to human intelligence was pioneered by Stanley Coren, author, neuropsychological researcher, and professor emeritus at the University of British Columbia. As part of an extensive study, he found dogs can solve complex spatial problems, including some requiring operating mechanisms such as the latch on a gate. He even found that, to achieve rewards, dogs can deliberately deceive both humans and other dogs.

The average dog is able to learn up to 165 words, and dogs with above-average intelligence can comprehend up to 250 words. They can also count to four or five and, amazingly, can usually even understand very basic math, such as one plus one equals two.

BRAINY BREEDS

Though intelligence varies among individual dogs, some breeds are known to be smarter than others. According to Coren, the smartest breeds are among the more newly developed, as opposed to ancient breeds; perhaps these dogs are seen as more intelligent because they are also more likely to be responsive to humans. Coren pointed to dogs as possessing three kinds of intelligence: instinctive (what a dog was originally developed to do, such as herding), adaptive (how a dog learns problem-solving from its environment), and working/obedience (what Coren calls "school learning").

SMARTEST DOG BREEDS (in order of intelligence)
1. Border collies
2. Poodles
3. German shepherds
4. Golden retrievers
5. Doberman pinschers (right)
6. Shetland sheepdogs
7. Labrador retrievers

With a vocabulary of more than 340 words, the border collie Betsy had above-average intelligence.

A border collie named Chaser is considered the smartest dog that has ever lived. Chaser was owned by a retired psychology professor who spent hours every day teaching her the names of toys and objects, keeping a journal so he himself could remember each toy's unique name. Before she passed away in 2019 at the age of 15, Chaser knew more than 1,000 words. According to Coren, Chaser's intelligence equivalency was about that of a three-year-old child. ◉

The intelligence of herding breeds—both purebred and mixes—helps them to excel at difficult jobs such as working on ranches and farms.

EXPLORING DOG EMOTIONS

Dogs do have feelings, but are they the same as ours?

Just a few decades ago, many scientists believed dogs didn't have the same range of emotional feelings as humans. The scientific community accepted that dogs experienced primal responses such as fear and anger, but scoffed at the notion of dogs feeling complex human emotions, including love. Recent research tells us otherwise.

In humans, different emotions develop over time, with basic emotions appearing first and more complex emotions developing later. Because dogs are, according to Coren, intellectually equivalent to a two- to three-year-old human, they likely have the same emotional capacities of a child of that age. This means that dogs experience the following basic emotions (listed here in chronological order of development): excitement/arousal, distress, contentment, disgust, fear, anger, joy, suspicion/shyness, and affection/love.

FAIR'S FAIR

Dogs are motivated by reward, but dogs will stop performing if they are not treated fairly, something called inequity aversion. In one experiment, researchers asked dogs to give a paw on command. The dogs were tested both individually and in pairs. Sometimes they were rewarded with a high-value treat (sausage) and other times with a low-value treat (bread). Sometimes they were not rewarded at all.

The dogs happily gave a paw almost every time when they were rewarded with treats and continued to do so relatively consistently (20 out of 30 requests), even if they didn't get a treat. But if one dog in a pair was rewarded and the other wasn't, the unrewarded dog stopped performing (only giving a paw 12 times out of 30). The dogs did not care if one dog received the sausage while the other got the bread—only the complete absence of a reward changed their behavior.

We used to think that dogs, such as this Belgian Tervuren (right), learned the concept of fairness from living with humans, but a new study has demonstrated that wolves also recognize fairness and stop performing quicker than dogs when favoritism is shown. It may be that domestication has made dogs less cooperative and more sensitive to hierarchy and status—with humans at the top of the pack.

Service dog Brew accompanies Vietnam War Navy veteran Tom Ellerd on California's Pacific Coast Highway in a scene for the IMAX film, *Superpower Dogs.*

It's easy for most dog owners to see evidence of many of these feelings in their pets, such as fear or anger. But because dogs can't talk to us, proving that they feel an emotion such as love is more difficult. Gregory Berns, neuroscientist and author of the book *What It's Like to Be a Dog,* has conducted several studies to reveal what's happening inside dog brains. The results suggest that dogs do feel positive, love-like emotions toward people, especially their owners.

In one of Berns's studies, dogs awake within an MRI machine were presented with different scents: their own, a familiar human, a strange human, a familiar dog, and a strange dog. Their caudate nucleus—a part of the brain that's associated with pleasure and emotion—lit up the most when the dogs smelled the scent of their owner. It appears that dogs can not only correctly identify their most familiar human's specific odor but also have a positive association with it.

That Guilty Look

We don't have any scientific evidence to prove that dogs *don't* feel complex emotions—anything is possible. But because children don't develop these more nuanced emotions until they are older than age two and a half, Coren thinks dogs are also unlikely to feel them, including guilt, shame, pride, and contempt.

Most dog owners dispute this, pointing to the classic "guilty look"—crouching body, head held low, eye peeping up—in a dog that has done something he

or she is not supposed to. Although it certainly *looks* like the dog is feeling the complex emotions of guilt and shame, you might be observing something else: fear and appeasement.

A study conducted by Alexandra Horowitz, an associate professor of psychology at Barnard College and author of the book *Inside of a Dog*, aimed to reveal what the guilty look in dogs represented. For the study, dogs and owners participated in a series of videotaped trials where the owner asked the dog not to eat a treat and then left the room. When the owners returned, they were told one of two

things: the dog disobeyed and ate the treat or the dog behaved and left the treat alone. However, the owners were not always told the truth, so some scolded their dogs when they did not eat the treat, and others praised their dogs when they did eat the treat.

The results? The researchers observed that dogs looked the most "guilty" when they were scolded by their owners—whether or not the dog had actually disobeyed. Dogs that *had* obeyed and not eaten the treat displayed the most guilty looks of all when they were scolded for doing something they did not do.

Horowitz concluded that the dogs were not giving "the look" because they felt guilt or shame. Instead, they were reacting to their owners' response about the incident. Attributing a dog's posture and actions to a complex human emotion such as guilt is a classic case of people anthropomorphizing—misreading dog behavior in human terms. It's especially easy to do this with dogs that we

Research shows that the "guilty look," such as the one from the border collie pup (above), is actually a dog's reaction to disapproval from people to whom the dog is bonded.

Photographer Seth Casteel's famous series on dogs underwater includes this exuberant black Labrador retriever (opposite) chasing her favorite tennis ball.

are closely bonded. But the more we learn about dog behavior and body language, the better we can understand our beloved companions.

Do Dogs Feel Empathy?

Empathy is another higher-level emotion that we may not expect dogs to have, but plenty of pet owners report that their dog comes over to comfort them when they're feeling sad or are crying. Studies have shown that dogs do respond to humans and other dogs in distress (for instance, by whimpering in response), and will even navigate their way past barriers to do so—but exactly *why* they do this is tricky to prove. Some scientists believe that dogs are not displaying true empathy but something called emotional contagion—responding to the emotions of another individual despite not truly understanding those feelings.

To test if dogs feel empathy or emotional contagion, two psychologists performed an experiment to see if dogs would react with empathy toward a stranger as well as their owner. In the study, the dogs observed their owner and a stranger either humming, talking, or crying. When the stranger pretended to cry, rather than approaching their owner (their usual source of comfort), most of the dogs nuzzled and licked the stranger instead, a response behaviorally consistent with empathic concern. It has also been documented that the higher the dog scored on a "bond test" (measuring their level of attachment to their owner), the faster they would try to reach their owner in distress.

Though this shows that dogs are sensitive to suffering in humans, we still don't know for sure that dogs can feel true empathy, which requires the ability to differentiate between "self" and "other" in a relationship, something we don't yet know if animals can do. ⊚

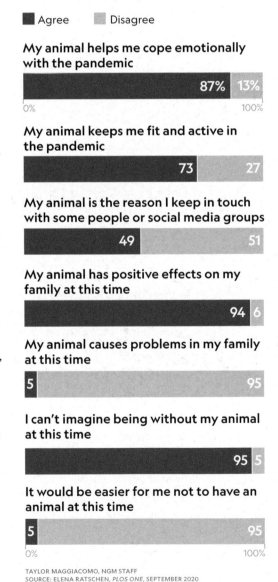

Animals are a source of emotional support during the COVID-19 pandemic.

■ Agree   ▪ Disagree

My animal helps me cope emotionally with the pandemic
87% 13%
0%   100%

My animal keeps me fit and active in the pandemic
73   27

My animal is the reason I keep in touch with some people or social media groups
49   51

My animal has positive effects on my family at this time
94   6

My animal causes problems in my family at this time
5   95

I can't imagine being without my animal at this time
95   5

It would be easier for me not to have an animal at this time
5   95
0%   100%

TAYLOR MAGGIACOMO, NGM STAFF
SOURCE: ELENA RATSCHEN, *PLOS ONE*, SEPTEMBER 2020

Dogs' charming, humanlike expressions endear them to us. Though this pup is enjoying his saunter down a Montana street, many places have leash laws for the protection of both dogs and people.

WRITTEN ALL OVER THEIR FACE

Whether pleading for a taste of your snack or simply gazing lovingly into your eyes, nothing tugs at the heartstrings quite like a dog's humanlike expressions. Dogs can move their eyebrows up and down, allowing them to mirror human expressions. Researchers discovered that domestic dogs such as this terrier mix (right) evolved to have a special muscle that allows them to do this, a muscle that wolves do not have. Scientists theorize that these facial expressions contribute to dogs' endearing juvenile appearance, which makes humans love them and want to nurture them.

What's more, dogs' facial expressions are not involuntary, as previously thought. Research has shown that dogs deliberately make certain facial expressions in attempting to communicate with humans to get what they want. In one study, dogs' facial movements were filmed as people offered or withheld treats, either facing the dog or turned away. The dogs made significantly more facial expressions when the human was facing them, including showing their tongues and raising their eyebrows. This suggests the dogs made these expressions on purpose to get the treat.

WHY DOGS NEED SOCIALIZATION

The importance of introducing your pet to the human world

If you've ever brought home a new puppy, you probably learned about the importance of socialization, which is a process of carefully introducing a young dog to the world in a positive way so it grows up to be confident rather than fearful.

Socialization ideally takes place during a puppy's first few months of life, from three to about 14 weeks old. This window of opportunity is when puppies are primed to explore and learn without excessive fear. Though researchers have documented that puppies go through an initial "fear period" between eight and 11 weeks of age, their curiosity overcomes their fear. During this time, expose your puppy to as many people, sights, and sounds as you can, keeping things positive.

Puppies should meet children and adults of all ages; play with vaccinated

Places of business, including an art house cinema (opposite) in Gothenburg, Sweden, are increasingly opening their doors to canine customers.

Socialization, the process of exposing young dogs to everyday sights and sounds, helps dogs gain the confidence to live happily in our human world.

DOGS AGE FASTER THAN HUMANS DO; MOST ARE **FULLY GROWN BY THEIR FIRST BIRTHDAY.**

and friendly dogs and puppies (organized puppy socialization classes are great for this); visit a variety of environments such as parks, beaches, and downtown areas; learn to ride in the car; listen to large trucks rumbling; see people riding bikes, scooters, and skateboards; hang out in dog-friendly restaurants and stores; and any other experiences you can think of.

Bring treats along to make positive connections to potentially frightening situations and let your puppy approach new things on its own. Go slow, trying not to overwhelm your puppy with too much too fast. If something "scary" does happen, avoid picking up your puppy or coddling it. The more a young dog learns to stand on its own four paws, the better its confidence will be. To reinforce everything the puppy is learning and experiencing, socialization should be continued throughout the puppy's first year of life.

A Fearful Time

If pups get appropriate socialization between three and 14 weeks of age—the golden socialization window—they are usually in a good position to work through any fears that crop up in the stronger fear period that happens later in puppyhood between roughly six to 14 months of age. Although it's possible to begin socializing puppies after 14 weeks old, it is more challenging. Older dogs can be socialized, but the process might take a lot longer and could require the help of a professional trainer or animal behaviorist.

Olive the Saint Bernard and Sophie the cat have grown up together. Dogs and cats can learn to get along when properly socialized to one another, especially if exposure happens at an early age.

Puppies lacking adequate socialization are in danger of growing up to be fearful of the outside world. They might be uncomfortable around new people and/or dogs, as well as reactive and sensitive to loud sounds. If you have an older puppy or adult dog that is acting scared, seek help as soon as possible from your veterinarian or an animal behaviorist. The sooner you intervene, the better the outcome will be. ◉

BODY LANGUAGE

Posture, position, and movement all have meaning

Humans, who mainly communicate through verbal language, tend to talk to dogs a lot. We know dogs can learn around 165 words, and we think they appreciate the nuances of our tone. Dogs might also like the sound of our voices, but they probably don't understand much of what we're saying to them. Likewise, we don't always understand what dogs are saying to us or to each other.

Canine communication takes place largely through nonverbal cues. Dogs are great at reading all sorts of body language, including that of other dogs and humans. But people aren't usually very skilled at reading dog body language. The good news is you can learn to recognize basic canine cues and, in doing so, learn to speak dog. Understanding how your dog is feeling provides great insight into your dog's emotional state and can even help you ward off unnecessary stress and behavioral issues.

Signs of a Relaxed, Happy Dog

Calm dogs have a relaxed body posture, with ears in a neutral position and eyes softened. Their mouth may be closed or open, with the dog softly panting. The tail is in a neutral position, either held still or wagging. If a very relaxed dog is lying down, the legs may splay out behind it (aptly termed "frog legs").

Signs of a Playful Dog

A playful dog may bounce around or move in an exaggerated manner, wagging its tail, barking spiritedly, and tossing or shaking a toy, perhaps while growling in a playful way. Play between

DID YOU KNOW?

DOGS **YAWN TO CALM THEMSELVES DOWN,** AS WELL AS WHEN THEY'RE TIRED.

Dogs have special ways of communicating with each other via their body language. In the image above, the dog's stance with chest down and rear raised signifies a desire to play.

Very relaxed dogs, such as the bulldog opposite, might lie with their legs stretched out behind them.

two dogs might seem intense, with lots of pouncing, wrestling, and vocalization, but if the dogs are not hurting each other and both keep going back for more, it's likely all in good fun. The ultimate sign of a dog ready to romp is what is called a "play bow," when a dog lowers the front half of its body down to the ground with its rear up in the air, tail wagging. This position, which inspired the downward dog pose in yoga, is an invitation to frolic or a request to keep a play session going.

Signs of a Deferential Dog

Dogs that are feeling unsure, or those that don't want to engage in contact or conflict with another dog, will display appeasement behaviors, sometimes called deferential behaviors, meant to communicate that they are not a threat. The best known of these is a dog showing its belly; other appeasement behaviors include avoiding eye contact, yawning, licking lips, lowering the head, turning away, holding the tail low or tucking it between the legs, crouching down, or raising one paw. Dogs generally exhibit these behaviors to decrease the possibility of conflict or attack from another dog. They are trying to say, "I'm not going to bother you, so please don't bother me." This type of behavior is sometimes described as submissive, especially when dogs act this way toward humans. A submissive dog that shows its belly is communicating that they recognize that human as a leader or authority figure.

Signs of an Aroused Dog

Arousal, a state of extreme excitement, can be recognized in a dog's stiff, erect body posture, with its hair standing up along the spine, ears up or forward, tail held up and stiffly wagging, often while barking and lunging. In dogs, a state of arousal can quickly progress to overexcitement and behavioral outbursts such as jumping up, mounting or humping, or mouthing (biting) a person's clothing or skin.

Signs of an Aggressive Dog

A dog's threatening body language is some of the easiest for humans to read. The message is loud and clear—stay away! A dog expresses aggression by

DOGS USE THEIR POSTURE TO COMMUNICATE, SHRINKING DOWN OR STANDING TALL TO CONVEY THEIR MEANING.

standing with a very stiff, rigid posture with a forward lean and giving a direct and challenging stare with wide-open eyes. Often, the dog will raise its hackles (called piloerection, where the hair stands up on the shoulders, neck, and back). The dog's ears may be pinned back or be held forward or to the side. Its lips are tight or even pulled back to show its teeth, and the dog may be growling or barking. The tail may also be held high like a flag, or low and stiff. Aggressive dogs often wag their tails, but it's a very stiff wagging, more like twitching. ◉

Dogs use many signs to warn people and other animals to stay away, including baring their teeth and growling.

Dogs in shelters are often stressed or fearful—only after adoption and adjustment to their new home do their true personalities shine.

FEAR IN DOGS

Some signs of fear in dogs are obvious, such as cowering, trembling, whining, or trying to hide or run away. But before they get too distressed, dogs display subtle signs that they are feeling uncomfortable. Learning to recognize small signs of worry or fear can help you intervene sooner in a situation, either removing your dog or removing the stressor.

Knowing your dog is uncomfortable with certain interactions can even ward off dog bites. One study had adults view videos of young children interacting with dogs, then had them classify how the dogs were feeling during the interactions. Although experts identified the dogs in the video as "fearful or anxious" and "lacking in confidence," a majority of the test subjects said the dogs looked relaxed (68.4 percent) and confident (65.1 percent), demonstrating that people have trouble gauging dog body language during child-dog interactions.

SOME OF THE MOST COMMON SIGNS OF FEAR IN DOGS INCLUDE
- Yawning
- Licking lips
- Drooling
- Panting
- Averting eyes, dilated pupils
- Showing whites of the eyes
- Turning head to the side
- Pinning ears back
- Tucking tail
- Whining
- Shivering/trembling
- Pacing
- Cowering
- Hiding/trying to escape
- Hair standing up on neck or back
- Growling or barking

CANINE COMMUNICATION

Dogs can "talk" to each other in a wide variety of ways

Dogs may not speak our language, but they do use vocalization to "talk" to other dogs, other animals, and people. And they send and receive a lot of information via scent—remember, a dog's sense of smell is as much as 100,000 times better than a human's.

Pee-Mail

For most dogs, one of the best parts of going for a walk around town is having the opportunity to send and receive messages to other animals in the area, jokingly referred to as checking their "pee-mail." Though people think of urine marking as a way for dogs to claim their territory, dogs can also gather and transmit an incredible amount of information simply by smelling another animal's pee and then peeing themselves.

With one sniff, dogs can detect different chemicals in left-behind urine that tell them another dog's age and sex, whether it is spayed or neutered, whether a female is in heat, and if the other dog is sick. Dogs can also identify the pee of dogs they know, as well as detect unfamiliar dogs or other animals. Some dogs will urinate on top of the pee they come across, called "overmarking"

or "countermarking." We don't know for sure why dogs do this, but some theorize it's in some way competitive, or related to mating. Any dog can scent mark, including females, but unneutered males are more likely to overmark an unspayed female dog's pee.

Male dogs also raise their legs so they can aim the stream of urine higher when marking vertical surfaces, such as

HOW TO TELL IF A DOG IS IN PAIN

Animals instinctually hide their pain or illness. In the wild, a sick or injured animal is a prime target to be picked off by a predator. For this reason, even if a dog is feeling poorly, it will often go about its daily life as if nothing is amiss. Thus, by the time a dog starts to show obvious signs of pain, its injury or illness may have progressed quite far. However, dogs do display many subtle signs of pain, if we pay close attention.

SOME COMMON SIGNS OF PAIN IN DOGS INCLUDE
- Shaking, shivering, or trembling
- Restlessness/can't settle down
- Stiff posture or arched back with head held low
- Panting, even when temperatures are cool and the dog is not exercising
- Yelping, growling, or biting when touched or picked up
- Refusal to jump as usual onto the couch or to climb stairs
- Difficulty standing up or lying down
- Not wanting to walk or play
- Eating or drinking less, or not at all

A North Dakota boy celebrates the expansion of his farm family. Puppies learn many skills from other dogs, but some skills are innate.

trees, mailbox posts, and fire hydrants. This makes it more likely other dogs will smell the pee and sends a message about the size of the dog who did the marking: The higher the pee, the bigger the dog. But small dogs have figured out a neat trick. According to one study, short dogs tend to hold their leg higher and lean back farther than tall dogs, making it seem that they are bigger based on the height of the urine mark.

Though it might feel annoying when your dog stops to sniff or pee every few feet while you're trying to go for a brisk stroll, consider giving your pup some time to check their pee-mail. The mental stimulation your dog gets from investigating these smells is just as important as the physical activity gained from walking.

Bark Talk

Though dogs don't use spoken language the way humans do, they are capable of making a variety of different vocalizations, including barking, howling, whining, and growling. Interpreting canine speak is a fine art. Dogs bark in different ways and for different reasons, expressing excitement, joy, fear, anxiety, suspicion, frustration, and anger, among other things. Dogs have also learned to bark at people to get something they want, whether food, a favorite toy, or simply attention.

Similarly, dogs whine for many reasons, and it's important to consider the context to figure out if the message is one of fear, pain, sadness, happiness, excitement, or to ask for food or

Small dogs often hike their legs up extra high as they deposit urine to leave the impression that they are bigger.

Some dogs, such as this one inside a Channel Islands pub, howl in response to music, as if they are singing along with the tune.

attention. A lot of dogs whine at the door to signal they're ready to relieve themselves outside. Although growling often serves as a warning to stay clear, many dogs growl when play-fighting with other dogs, or during a game of tug, or when "killing" a fluffy squeaky toy.

Howling usually means a dog is feeling scared or lonely, because howling is an instinctive way of trying to communicate with other members of the pack. Dogs left alone for long periods of time might resort to howling. Hearing fire or police sirens can also trigger howling, possibly because the dog thinks it's hearing another dog in the distance.

Some breeds make very specific, unique sounds that other breeds don't. Scent hound breeds such as bloodhounds, beagles, and coonhounds, make a unique

A DOG CAN MAKE ABOUT 100 DIFFERENT FACIAL EXPRESSIONS.

sound known as a bay—a long, deep, loud *ahhh-roooo!* Baying is often heard when hunting dogs are on the scent and tracking prey, but hounds might bay at home just for fun. The basenji, known as the "barkless breed" because it doesn't bark in the traditional sense, does make sounds, including yodeling. The New Guinea singing dog is so named because it modulates its vocalizations. The Shiba Inu may scream when it doesn't like what's going on, and the Siberian husky can make vocalizations that sound a lot like human language. ◉

LIVING WITH HUMANS

Training helps dogs and their people happily coexist

To coexist peacefully with people, dogs must learn how to live in a human world. Many natural dog behaviors such as barking, nipping, digging, chewing, and escaping are undesirable to humans. Dogs aren't born knowing that we prefer that they pee and poop outside, or that jumping up is not an acceptable way of showing affection. This is where training comes in.

Pet owners can set their dogs up for success by demonstrating exactly what they expect from day one. Consistency in house rules goes a long way toward raising a well-behaved dog that is a pleasure to live with. It's easier to show your dog what you expect of them than to let them make mistakes and have to retrain behaviors you don't want.

Dogs respond incredibly well to positive reinforcement. For many decades dog training was heavy-handed, but science has shown that aversive-based training using punishment is not only less effective than positive training but also harmful to dogs' long-term welfare. Though most dogs inherently want to please, some breeds are more stubborn and independent. However, almost any dog can be motivated—you just need to identify what your dog finds rewarding.

Agility training includes jumping through tires and over hurdles, racing through tunnels, weaving through poles, and stopping on command, all offering dogs both physical exercise and mental stimulation.

HELP FOR BEHAVIOR PROBLEMS

Undesirable behavior is the most common reason people surrender their dogs to animal shelters, yet most of these habits can be addressed with the assistance of an experienced trainer and/or animal behaviorist. The key is to get help as early as possible; as with people, the more ingrained a dog's actions are, the harder it is to eliminate them.

SOME OF THE MOST COMMON BEHAVIORAL ISSUES IN DOGS INCLUDE

- Digging
- Escaping
- Barking
- Mouthing/biting
- Separation anxiety
- Jumping up on people
- Destructive chewing (right)
- Food/resource guarding
- Aggression toward other dogs or humans

School Is in Session

Once you're sure your new puppy or dog is healthy and has at least its first set of vaccines, one of the best ways to help achieve behavioral success is by enrolling in a training class. In addition to private trainers, many communities offer classes through their parks and recreation department. Both often offer safe and supervised socialization through organized classes or "puppy kindergarten," which also teach the basics of learning to sit, lie down, and stay. It's helpful to have an instructor who can intervene and redirect if play gets too rough.

DOGS HAVE A SENSE OF TIME.

Obedience classes teach your older puppy or dog more advanced skills; these may include long stays, recalls, retrieving, and loose-leash walking. Other types of classes include trick training, agility, nose work, and more. These varied activities are fun for both dogs and their people, offering mental and physical exercise as well as bonding time as you and your dog achieve goals together.

Life with dogs is sometimes challenging, but it helps to understand where they come from, why they act the way they do, and even learn how they're thinking and feeling. Discovering the secrets of a dog's world can reduce miscommunication, strengthen your bond, and bring your relationship to a new level. ◉

At a minimum, all dogs need daily walks, and some breeds—including herding dogs, sporting breeds, and working dogs—require more vigorous exercise to burn off excess energy.

THE SECRET LIFE OF DOGS
Jackie Brown

PRODUCED BY
NATIONAL GEOGRAPHIC PARTNERS, LLC
1145 17th Street NW
Washington, DC 20036-4688 USA

ISSN 2160-7141

Published by Meredith Operations Corporation
225 Liberty Street • New York, NY 10281

Printed in the USA

NATIONAL GEOGRAPHIC MEDIA
David E. Miller, EVP & General Manager
Nathan Lump, SVP & Editorial Director
David Brindley, Managing Editor, Magazines
John MacKethan, Director, Print Operations

NEWSSTAND SPECIAL ISSUES
SENIOR PHOTO EDITOR Breann Birkenbuel
SENIOR EDITOR Lori Cuthbert
SENIOR EDITORIAL MANAGER Bridget E. Hamilton
SENIOR PRODUCTION EDITOR Alexandra Hartnett
DESIGN EDITOR Linda Makarov

CARTOGRAPHY
EDITOR Rosemary P. Wardley

MANUFACTURING & DISTRUBUTION
PRODUCTION MANAGER Jennifer Hoff
GLOBAL RETAIL MANAGER Suzanne H. Mackay
SENIOR MANAGER Kristin M. Semeniuk

PRODUCTION SERVICES
DIRECTOR/ADMIN Bill Reicherts
IMAGING SPECIALISTS Rahsaan Jackson, Wendy K. Smith

Special thanks to Marshall Kiker, Mary Norris, and
Katherine Shaw.

Dedicated to my beloved miniature poodle
Jäger (2009-2022), forever in my heart.—JB

Become a *National Geographic* subscriber by using
your smartphone's camera to scan the QR code below:

ILLUSTRATIONS CREDITS

Cover, Vincent J. Musi; 0–1, Keith Ladzinski; 2–3, Keith Ladzinski;
4, Karine Aigner; 4–5, Maria Stenzel/National Geographic
Image Collection; 6–7, Ronan Donovan/National Geographic
Image Collection; 8, © NPL - DeA Picture Library/Bridgeman
Images; 9, Robert Clark/National Geographic Image Collection;
10, Vincent J. Musi/National Geographic Image Collection;
11 (LO), Joel Sartore/National Geographic Photo Ark; 11 (UP),
Ronan Donovan/National Geographic Image Collection; 12,
The Royal Belgian Institute of Natural Sciences, Brussels; 12–13,
Richard Barnes/National Geographic Image Collection; 14,
Del Baston, courtesy of the Center for American Archeology;
15, Keith Ladzinski; 16, Image courtesy of NHGRI; 17, Richard
Barnes/National Geographic Image Collection; 18, bonzami
emmanuelle/Alamy Stock Photo; 19, Giuseppe Nucci; 20, Keith
Ladzinski/National Geographic Image Collection; 21, Johan
Nilsson/TT News Agency/AFP/Getty Images; 23, Vincent J. Musi/
National Geographic Image Collection; 24–25, Vincent J. Musi/
National Geographic Image Collection; 26, Pablo Corral Vega/
National Geographic Image Collection; 29, Robert Clark/National
Geographic Image Collection; 30–31, Catherine Karnow/National
Geographic Image Collection; 32–33, Adam Ferguson/National
Geographic Image Collection; 34, Gabriele Maerz/Alamy Stock
Photo; 35, Rebecca Hale/National Geographic Image Collection;
36–37, Jim Richardson/National Geographic Image Collection;
46, Nancy Borowick; 38–39, Mark Thiessen/National Geographic
Image Collection; 40–41, Esther Horvath; 42, Tomas Munita;
43, Martin Schoeller/National Geographic Image Collection;
44, Ami Vitale; 45 (LO), Joel Sartore/National Geographic
Photo Ark; 45 (UP), Matthieu Paley/National Geographic Image
Collection; 46, Nancy Borowick; 47, Dina Litovsky; 48–49, Nancy
Borowick; 49, GlobalP/iStock/Getty Images Plus; 51, Ami Vitale;
52, Joel Sartore/National Geographic Image Collection; 54–55,
Robert Clark/National Geographic Image Collection; 56–57,
Graham Swain/EyeEm/Getty Images; 58–59, Mariceu Erthal
García; 60, Julie Nichol/Alamy Stock Photo; 60–61, Ami Vitale;
62–63, Randy Olson/National Geographic Image Collection; 64,
Elena Elisseeva/Alamy Stock Photo; 65, Robert Andrew Richter/
National Geographic Image Collection; 66–67, Nancy Borowick;
68–69, Jasper Doest/National Geographic Image Collection;
70, WilleeCole/Alamy Stock Photo; 71, Vincent J. Musi/National
Geographic Image Collection; 72–73, Joel Sartore/National
Geographic Image Collection; 74, Angelique van Heertum/
Alamy Stock Photo; 74–75, Danny Wilcox Frazier/VII; 76, Seth
Casteel/National Geographic Image Collection; 77, Erik Lam/
Alamy Stock Photo; 79 (LO), Joel Sartore/National Geographic
Image Collection; 79 (UP), Keith Ladzinski; 80, Karine Aigner; 81,
Nora Lorek; 82–83, Ami Vitale; 84, blickwinkel/Alamy Stock Photo;
84–85, Chiara Goia; 86, Robbie George/National Geographic
Image Collection; 87, Katie Orlinsky; 89, Jim Richardson/National
Geographic Image Collection; 90, Paolo Cremonesi/iStock/
Getty Images Plus; 91, James L. Amos/National Geographic
Image Collection; 92, Life on white/Alamy Stock Photo; 93, Anne
Maenurm/National Geographic Image Collection; 94–95, Aaron
Huey/National Geographic Image Collection; 97, Vincent J. Musi.

Opposite: Dogs, such as this wire fox terrier, have learned to live
happily in a human world, stealing our hearts along the way.